SCIENCE FICTION

Essential Literary Genres

BY SUSAN E. HAMEN

Essential Library

An Imprint of Abdo Publishing | abdopublishing.com

ABDOPUBLISHING.COM

Published by Abdo Publishing, a division of ABDO, PO Box 398166, Minneapolis, Minnesota 55439. Copyright © 2017 by Abdo Consulting Group, Inc. International copyrights reserved in all countries. No part of this book may be reproduced in any form without written permission from the publisher. Essential Library™ is a trademark and logo of Abdo Publishing.

Printed in the United States of America, North Mankato, Minnesota
102016
012017

**THIS BOOK CONTAINS
RECYCLED MATERIALS**

Interior Photos: Milbert Orlando Brown/KRT/Newscom, 10–11; Timothy H. O'Sullivan/ Library of Congress, 13; Photo12/UIG/Getty Images, 17; AP Images, 21, 36, 46–47; William Still, Louise A. Smith, J. W. Eaton, and E. Cornish, 25; Everett Collection, 35; ABC/ Photofest, 40; Pictorial Press Ltd/Alamy, 43; Mary Evans/Ronald Grant/Everett Collection, 51; Ed Kashi/Liaison/Hulton Archive/Getty Images, 59; Touchstone/Everett Collection, 61, 64, 69, 71, 75; Admedia, Inc/Byron Purvis/AdMedia/Sipa USA/Newscom, 83; Chuck Zlotnick/©Columbia Pictures/Everett Collection, 85, 90–91, 96

Editor: Arnold Ringstad
Series Designer: Maggie Villaume

PUBLISHER'S CATALOGING-IN-PUBLICATION DATA

Names: Hamen, Susan E., author.
Title: Science fiction / by Susan E. Hamen.
Description: Minneapolis, MN : Abdo Publishing, 2017. | Series: Essential
    literary genres | Includes bibliographical references and index.
Identifiers: LCCN 2016945477 | ISBN 9781680783834 (lib. bdg.) |
    ISBN 9781680797367 (ebook)
Subjects: LCSH: Literature--Juvenile literature. | Literary form--Juvenile
    literature.
Classification: DDC 809--dc23
LC record available at http://lccn.loc.gov/2016945477

CONTENTS

INTRODUCTION TO
LITERARY GENRES

Why do we read and write literature? Telling stories is an integral part of being human, a universal experience across history and cultures. Literature as we know it today is the written form of these stories and ideas. Writing allows authors to take their readers on a journey that crosses the boundaries of space and time. Literature allows us to understand the experiences of others and express experiences of our own.

What Is a Genre?

A genre is a specific category, or type, of literature. Broad genres of literature include nonfiction, poetry, drama, and fiction. Smaller groupings include subject-based genres such as mystery, science fiction, romance, or fantasy. Literature can also be classified by its audience, such as young adult (YA) or children's, or its format, such as a graphic novel or picture book.

What Are Literary Theory and Criticism?

Literary theory gives us tools to help decode a text. On one level, we can examine the words and phrases the author uses so we can interpret or debate his or her message. We can ask questions about how the book's structure creates an effect on the reader, and whether this is the effect the author intended. We can analyze symbolism or themes in a work. We can dive deeper by asking how a work either supports or challenges society and its values or traditions.

You can look at these questions using different criticisms, or schools of thought. Each type of criticism asks you to look at the work from a different perspective. Perhaps you want to examine what the work says about the writer's life or the time period in which the work was created. Biographical or historical criticism considers these questions. Or perhaps you are interested in what the work says about the role of women or the structure of society. Feminist or Marxist theories seek to answer those types of questions.

How Do You Apply Literary Criticism?

You write an analysis when you use a literary or critical approach to examine and question a work. The theory you choose is a lens through which you can view the work, or a springboard for asking questions about the work. Applying a theory helps you think critically. You are free to question the work and make an assertion about it. If you choose to examine a work using racial criticism, for example, you may ask questions about how the work challenges or upholds racial structures in society. Or you may ask how a character's race affects his or her identity or development throughout the work.

Forming a Thesis

Form your questions and find answers in the work or other related materials. Then you can create a thesis. The thesis is the key point in your analysis. It is your argument about the work based on the school of thought you are using. For example, if you want to approach a work using feminist criticism, you could write the following thesis: The character of Margy in Sissy Johnson's *Margy Sings the Blues* uses her songwriting to subvert traditional gender roles.

HOW TO MAKE A THESIS STATEMENT

In an analysis, a thesis statement typically appears at the end of the introductory paragraph. It is usually only one sentence long and states the author's main idea.

Providing Evidence

Once you have formed a thesis, you must provide evidence to support it. Evidence will usually take the form of examples and quotations from the work itself, often including dialogue from a character. You may wish to address what others have written about the work. Quotes from these individuals may help support your claim. If you find any quotes or examples that contradict your thesis, you will need to create an argument against them. For instance: Many critics claim Margy's actions uphold traditional gender roles, even if her songs went against them. However, the novel's resolution proves Margy had the power to change society through her music.

HOW TO SUPPORT A THESIS STATEMENT

An analysis should include several arguments that support the thesis's claim. An argument is one or two sentences long and is supported by evidence from the work being discussed. Organize the arguments into paragraphs. These paragraphs make up the body of the analysis.

Concluding the Essay

After you have written several arguments and included evidence to support them, finish the essay with a conclusion. The conclusion restates the ideas from the

HOW TO CONCLUDE AN ESSAY

Begin your conclusion with a recap of the thesis and a brief summary of the most important or strongest arguments. Leave readers with a final thought that puts the essay in a larger context or considers its wider implications.

thesis and summarizes some of the main points from the essay. The conclusion's final thought often considers additional implications for the essay or gives the reader something to ponder further.

In This Book

In this book, you will read summaries of works, each followed by an analysis. Critical thinking sections will give you a chance to consider other theses and questions about the work. Did you agree with the author's analysis? What other questions are raised by the thesis and its arguments? You can also see other directions the author could have pursued to analyze the work. Then, in the Analyze It section in the final pages of this book, you will have an opportunity to create your own analysis paper.

Science Fiction

The works covered in this book are from the science fiction genre. The term *science fiction* was first used in 1851. But its earliest roots are in fantasy, a genre that includes stories containing supernatural elements. Ovid's *Metamorphoses*, written in 8 CE, and the Old English epic poem *Beowulf*, written between the 700s and 1000s CE, contain science fiction–like elements.

Medieval literature has many examples of early science fiction–type stories, but the genre began gaining popularity in the late 1800s with authors such as Jules Verne and H. G. Wells. Verne's stories mixed adventure and technology, catapulting science fiction into popularity. Wells used his science fiction novels to make statements about society, tackling such themes as power, war, community, and exile.

Science fiction includes many common themes, including alien invasion and abduction, space exploration, and time travel. Science fiction literature can be entertaining, but it can also present the reader with opportunities to explore and reflect on how humans relate to the universe in which they live.

LOOK FOR THE GUIDES

Throughout the chapters that analyze the works, thesis statements have been highlighted. The box next to the thesis helps explain what questions are being raised about the work. Supporting arguments have also been highlighted. The boxes next to the arguments help explain how these points support the thesis. The conclusions are also accompanied by explanatory boxes. Look for these guides throughout each analysis.

2

AN OVERVIEW OF
KINDRED

Octavia Butler's *Kindred,* first published in 1979, tells the story of a young African-American woman living in California in the late 1970s. Through an unexplained phenomenon, the story's protagonist is repeatedly transported back to the era of her ancestors in the pre–Civil War (1861–1865) South. There, she experiences life on a slave planation as she struggles to survive and return to her own time.

An Ancestral Bond

The story opens on June 9, 1976. Dana is celebrating her twenty-sixth birthday as she and her husband, Kevin Franklin, a white man, move from Los Angeles, California,

into a suburban house in Altadena, California. As they unpack and begin to settle into their new home, Dana suddenly feels dizzy. She falls to her knees as the room blurs. Kevin moves toward her, but just as she gasps, "Something is wrong with me," her surroundings, including Kevin, disappear.[1] She finds herself transported to a grove of trees near a river. Dana hears a child drowning. She runs into the water and hauls out a boy who is approximately four or five years old. She tries to revive him by pushing on his chest, but a woman Dana assumes is the boy's mother panics and tries to pull Dana away. Dana succeeds in resuscitating the red-haired boy and learns his name is Rufus. But his father arrives and aims a gun at Dana. She experiences another dizzy spell and finds herself transported back to her house in 1976. Kevin claims she was gone for only a few seconds. However, to Dana, it was as if she were gone for several minutes.

Dana has just enough time to shower before she is again transported back to Rufus, who is now in his bedroom and a few years older. Rufus is once again in peril, having set his bedroom drapes on fire in a fit of anger toward his father. Dana extinguishes the fire and learns from Rufus that the year is 1815 and they are on a plantation in Maryland. Dana bristles at the boy's casual use of the word *nigger* and asks him to refer to her as a black woman. Dana pieces together that Rufus and his father, Tom Weylin, are her ancestors. Dana remembers that Rufus Weylin and a black girl named Alice had a daughter in 1831 named Hagar Weylin, her great-grandmother. Rufus remembers Dana from the previous incident at the river and sends her to the home of Alice Greenwood so she will not be caught by his father.

She arrives to find a group of young white men beating Alice's father and mother. Once they leave, Dana tries to help the woman, but one of the men returns. He assumes Dana is a runaway slave and attempts to rape her. Fearing for her life, she experiences another dizzy spell and is pulled back to her own time.

Dana is shocked to find herself back in the era of American slavery.

Dana awakens to Kevin's voice. The two grapple to make sense of her time traveling. Kevin ties a tote bag around Dana's waist containing some extra clothing and a switchblade. The two research as much as they can about slavery. Kevin points out that both times she feared for her life in the past, she experienced a dizzy spell and returned to 1976. Dana suspects she is drawn back to the past whenever Rufus's life is in danger.

Life on a Plantation

The next time Dana time travels, she pulls Kevin, who was holding on to her at the time, along with her. They find Rufus, who has broken his leg from a fall out of a tree. They send a slave boy named Nigel to fetch Tom Weylin. Dana talks with Rufus as they wait and ends up telling him she is from the future. Kevin shows Rufus some coins from his pocket stamped with the year 1965. Rufus suggests they tell people Dana is Kevin's slave, pointing out, "That's better than saying you're his wife. Nobody would believe that."[2]

At Rufus's insistence, Kevin and Dana are invited by Tom Weylin to remain on the plantation and the couple end up staying for weeks. Dana assists a middle-age slave named Sarah in the cookhouse and becomes friendly with the other house slaves. They all comment on her peculiar clothing, and Nigel questions, "Why you try to talk like white folks?"[3] Dana lies and says she is a free black woman from New York, and that her mother was a teacher. They warn her about Tom Weylin, telling her he is already resentful about the educated manner in which she speaks and the fact that she's from a Free State. He fears she will give his slaves ideas about freedom. Later, Sarah tells Dana that "Marse Tom," or Master Tom, sold off three of her four children, leaving her with only her daughter Carrie.

While Kevin has accepted a tutoring position for Rufus, Dana settles into a pattern of doing household chores and reading to Rufus as he heals. She hopes she can have a positive influence on Rufus and perhaps turn him away from being a cruel slave owner like his father.

Dana has a number of run-ins with Rufus's mother, Margaret, who appears to be jealous of her ability to read as well as the respect and affection Dana gets from Rufus. In addition, Margaret has taken an interest in Kevin, who repeatedly declines her advances. Margaret's contempt is evident when she throws hot coffee on Dana. Kevin insists Dana should start sleeping with him in his room instead of with the other slaves in the attic.

Tom Weylin forces the slaves to witness the whipping of another slave who talked back. It serves as a cruel reminder to Dana about the time and place in which she is trapped. Later, Sarah reveals to Dana her hatred for Margaret, telling Dana that it was Margaret's idea to sell her three sons. After Tom Weylin's first wife, Miss Hannah, died, he married Margaret, who wanted new furniture, dishes, and other fancy things. According to Sarah, Hannah's things "[weren't] good enough for white-trash Margaret. So she made Marse Tom sell my three boys to get money to buy things she didn't even need!"[4]

Not long after, Tom Weylin catches Dana teaching Nigel to read in the cookhouse and whips her. Screaming, Dana tries to crawl away from the searing pain of the whip. She sees Kevin running toward her but passes out before he can reach her. She awakens in her home in 1976, alone.

The Horrors of Slavery

Eight days later, she is once again pulled back to Rufus. This time, he is approximately 19 years old and is being beaten by Alice's now husband, a slave named Isaac, because Rufus raped Alice. Dana prevents Isaac from

Slaves were sold at auctions in the pre–Civil War South.

killing Rufus, pointing out the ramifications should they be caught. Dana allows Isaac and Alice to run away while she helps get Rufus home. Rufus confides that he is in love with Alice.

At the house, an aging Tom Weylin asks Dana to "take care of [Rufus]. . . . That seems to be what you're for, anyway."[5] He tells Dana that Kevin has left Maryland for the North.

Isaac and Alice are caught. Alice is beaten severely and mauled by dogs. Rufus buys her and brings her back to the house, imploring Dana to help her. When she is healed, he forces Dana to convince Alice to allow him to sleep with her. When Dana discovers that Rufus never sent letters she wrote to Kevin, she becomes angry and tries to run away. Rufus and his father find her, beat her, and have her whipped. As Dana is healing, Alice tells her

Kevin is on the way. Tom Weylin wrote him to tell him Dana had returned.

Not long after, Kevin, who has been trapped in the past for five years, rides up on a horse. Dana and Kevin immediately leave, but on the road, they meet up with Rufus, who begins firing shots at them. They both make it safely back to 1976.

The couple is home for only a few days before Dana is again transported back in time. This time, Rufus has malaria. Dana nurses him back to health, but he remains weak for days. When Dana is unable to save Tom Weylin's life after he suffers a heart attack, Rufus blames her and sends her to work in the fields. There, she is repeatedly whipped for not cutting corn fast enough and finally collapses.

As Dana is healing, Alice gives birth to Hagar, Dana's direct ancestor. Dana feels relieved that she has saved Rufus enough times to finally secure the birth of her great-grandmother. When Rufus beats her for interfering with the sale of some slaves, she slits her own wrists to force herself to fear for her life, and she is returned to Kevin in her own time.

The Final Farewell

When Dana next returns to the plantation, Alice has hanged herself. Rufus is racked with guilt over her death. In the library, Rufus and Dana discuss Alice and Dana's coming and going. Rufus tells her, "You were one woman. You and her. One woman. Two halves of a whole."[6] Dana, uncomfortable, leaves the library and heads up to her bag in the attic. She plans on slitting her wrists again to return home. Rufus follows Dana. He apologizes to her for the very first time, but then he attempts to rape her. Dana defends herself but ends up stabbing Rufus to death. He falls down on top of her, still holding her arm. She is transported home, but a crushing pain encircles her arm where Rufus's fingers are. She appears in her house missing her arm below the elbow.

After Dana is released from the hospital, she and Kevin fly to Maryland. They find nothing at the spot where the Weylin house used to stand, and they learn it was destroyed by a fire. Dana and Kevin both agree that hopefully now that Rufus is dead, there will be no more time traveling.

3

TIME TRAVEL AND THE FIGHT FOR RACIAL EQUALITY

Critical race theory (CRT) examines the issue of race or racism across literature, songs, film, and other modes of expression. It calls on the reader, listener, or viewer to consider how society and culture shape how people perceive, experience, and respond to race and racism.

Some of the questions CRT asks and explores include: How does race appear in US culture and affect how people interact with each other? How is racism reflected in books, songs, and film? How does racism continue to persist in US society? How can racism effectively be combated, and how can the experiences of victims of racism accurately be represented? Critical race theorists argue racism affects all members of

The civil rights movement of the 1950s and 1960s helped bring themes of racial equality into the national spotlight.

society, regardless of their racial identities. CRT also asserts race is an invention of society, rather than a physical or scientific classification.

In the 1970s, the era immediately following the civil rights movement, African-American author Octavia Butler emerged as a popular science fiction writer. She broke new ground in the genre, which up until her time had been almost exclusively dominated by white male authors. Butler's stories, including *Kindred*, blended elements of science fiction with issues of race, sex, and power. Butler's novels boldly explored people's attitudes about race and provided a context through which modern racial issues could be investigated and discussed.

During and after the civil rights movement, many African Americans rallied for equal rights. Butler pointed out in an interview that during that time many African Americans were ashamed of the treatment their parents and grandparents endured, as well as the lowly positions in which they were willing to work. She stated *Kindred* was a social, moral, and historical statement that allowed the reader to imagine how life was for these ancestors. Yet, the text also addressed racism in her modern-day 1970s. Butler's *Kindred* uses time travel to send a modern character back in time to experience slavery. In doing so, the author provides both the protagonist and the reader a better understanding of the forces of human behavior that made African Americans victims of slavery and racial inequality in the past and in the present.

Butler shows no amount of reading and research can equip Dana with the knowledge necessary to endure life as an African-American woman in the early 1800s. Dana is a modern-day woman who is educated and articulate. Unlike the slaves at the plantation, she can read and write. Although she has the benefit of knowing the history and brutality of slavery, she is ill-prepared for it when she is pulled back in time. During her brief returns to her modern-day home, she reads as much as she can to educate herself and better prepare to live as an African American in the pre–Civil War South.

On Dana's second trip to the past, she knows the perilous situation she is in as she makes her way through the night to the Greenwood home. She is aware she may be caught and assumed to be a runaway slave. Later in the story, Dana does run away after she discovers Rufus never sent her letters to Kevin. Although she had studied a map of the area and knew where she wanted to go, she is caught within hours. In contrast, Alice, with a limited education, was able to elude capture for days. Before beating and whipping her, Tom Weylin points out, "Educated nigger don't mean smart nigger, do it?"[1] As Dana is healing after her brutal whipping, she ponders, "Nothing in my education or knowledge of the future had helped me to escape. Yet in a few years an illiterate runaway named Harriet Tubman would make nineteen trips into this country and lead three hundred fugitives to freedom."[2] Despite her college-level education and research, Dana is no more prepared to try to escape than the slaves of the 1800s. Realizing this, she decides after her second whipping that she will submit to her slave status and not try to escape again.

Although Dana possesses certain skills that saved Rufus's life, and other skills that are valuable to Tom Weylin and Rufus at the plantation, these are not enough to prevent her from experiencing torture and assault at their hands. Rufus is aware early on that Dana is from the future and arrives to save his life. Dana prevents Rufus from drowning and burning, comes to

ARGUMENT TWO

The author next argues: "Although Dana possesses certain skills that saved Rufus's life, and other skills that are valuable to Tom Weylin and Rufus at the plantation, these are not enough to prevent her from experiencing torture and assault at their hands."

Thousands of slaves escaped the harsh world of slavery.

his aid when he breaks his leg, prevents him from being killed by Isaac, and nurses him through malaria. Rufus trusts Dana's medical knowledge, and Tom Weylin realizes Dana's purpose is to protect Rufus. Tom Weylin also asks Dana whether she knows how to do math, so he must have pondered putting her modern-day skills to further use. Yet, even though both Rufus and his father know she has repeatedly saved Rufus and could assist with intellectual tasks on the plantation, they still do not hesitate to hurt her like the slaves.

Butler addresses the themes of power and oppression that further trap African Americans in slavery by depicting the power struggle between the classes of slaves. The house slaves, although still trapped within the bonds of slavery, lead a much better existence than the field hands. They are treated better, receive better food, have more comfortable lodging, and they are not forced to work hard manual labor in the hot sun. When it is decided there is not enough work to justify two slaves sewing for the house,

ARGUMENT THREE

Here, the author addresses the power struggle within the institution of slavery: "Butler addresses the themes of power and oppression that further trap African Americans in slavery by depicting the power struggle between the classes of slaves."

Liza is sent to the fields, whereas Alice, Rufus's favorite, is allowed to stay. This prompts Liza to seek revenge, telling Rufus when Dana, Alice's friend, tries to escape. Dana is caught and whipped as a result. Dana points out:

> I was startled. I had never had a serious enemy—
> someone who would go out of her way to get me hurt
> or killed. To slaveholders and patrollers, I was just one
> more nigger, worth so many dollars. What they did
> to me didn't have much to do with me personally. But
> here was a woman who hated me and who, out of sheer
> malice, had nearly killed me.[3]

As punishment for Liza's betrayal, the other slaves beat her severely. Alice reassures Dana, "She'll keep her mouth shut next time. We let her know what would happen if she didn't. Now she's more scared of us than of Mister Tom."[4] In a world where slaves were suffering common injustices, the ordinary human emotions of jealousy and revenge remained. This led them to an inter-slave power struggle that resulted in the betrayal of a fellow slave.

The novel demonstrates through many examples

ARGUMENT FOUR

The author continues her argument with: "The novel demonstrates through many examples that slaves were forced to accept their positions to avoid further physical and emotional pain."

that slaves were forced to accept their positions to avoid further physical and emotional pain. Butler offers many examples of the cruel treatment the plantation owners and patrolmen doled out to African Americans, including both slaves and freemen. Alice's father, a slave, is beaten savagely, and her mother, a free woman, is also assaulted at the whim of young white men. Later, Alice is mauled by dogs and beaten after she tries to escape. Her husband's ears are cut off and he is sold. Many other slaves are tortured, beaten, whipped, and raped as punishment for infractions that include things as simple as reading. Luke fails to obey Tom Weylin and, as a consequence is separated from his family and sold. The only way the slaves are able to avoid such treatment is by doing exactly as they are told and avoiding all conflict with their masters.

For the slave mothers, survival isn't enough. They are forced to accept their slavery to protect their children. One example of this is the cook, Sarah. She absolutely loathes Miss Margaret, the woman responsible for selling her three boys to buy unnecessary finery for the house. But she buries her pain and resentment and accepts her fate as a slave, working hard to protect her remaining daughter, Carrie.

Butler doesn't stop at illustrating the atrocities the slaves endured in the 1800s. She challenges the reader to confront the lingering lack of equal rights afforded to African Americans in her 1970s. Kevin, Dana's husband, is a white man who defies convention and marries an African-American woman, despite his family's disapproval. Kevin's sister, who is married to a racist dentist, tells Kevin she will not allow the couple into her house if they marry.

Throughout the book, Butler makes it clear that African Americans in the pre–Civil War South had few options but to submit to slavery. To fight and to run usually ended in being whipped, tortured, mutilated, or raped. By allowing the protagonist, Dana, to endure this same treatment, the audience sees the futility of rebellion or escape. Even the most valued slave on a plantation was not above being beaten if the master felt like doing so. Rufus realizes Dana's rudimentary medical skills are better than their doctor's, yet he allows her to be whipped. Butler also demonstrates that, although

ARGUMENT FIVE

The author's final example addresses attitudes about race in her present-day United States: "Butler doesn't stop at illustrating the atrocities the slaves endured in the 1800s. She challenges the reader to confront the lingering lack of equal rights afforded to African Americans in her 1970s."

African Americans might not be subjected to slavery in the 1970s, attitudes about race still negatively affect modern-day society. Sarah's words to Dana about the situation they are in as blacks sadly sum up the reality of slavery and racism: "Don't matter what ought to be. Matters what is."[5]

CONCLUSION

The final paragraph concludes the author's analysis and sums up the arguments that support the thesis.

THINKING
CRITICALLY

Now it's your turn to assess the essay. Consider these questions:

1. The thesis statement argues that *Kindred* shows some of the forces that helped create and sustain the practice of slavery. Do you agree with this argument? Why or why not?

2. How does the essay draw a connection between the racist attitudes of the 1800s and those in the 1970s?

3. The conclusion should restate the thesis and the main arguments of the essay. Does the conclusion do so effectively? Explain.

OTHER

APPROACHES

There are several ways to approach a work of literature. You have read one way to think about the issues of slavery in *Kindred*. Other analyses could consider the text using different lenses. Here are two other ways a reader could look at the story.

Exploring Dana through a Feminist Lens

Feminist critique seeks to explore how female characters are portrayed in a work. This type of critique may examine whether women are depicted as fitting into a stereotypical role, such as a mother, a beautiful maiden, or an awkward bookworm. Dana is an intelligent young woman who is subjected to the brutal treatment of Rufus and his father in a different time period. She is also nearly raped. A possible thesis for exploring the role of Dana throughout the story and the ways in which she is treated might be: Despite the misogyny and sexism Dana experiences at the hands of Rufus and Tom Weylin, Dana emerges as a strong character who proves her power over these men.

A Historical Critique

Historical criticism looks at the historical and social circumstances of the time when a work was created. It then analyzes how the work was influenced by the time in which it was produced.

When *Kindred* was written, the United States had just experienced the civil rights movement, and many African Americans became active in the Black Power Movement. African Americans felt a renewed sense of racial pride and began exploring their history in depth. Butler wrote *Kindred* as a social commentary, helping her fellow African Americans understand what life might have been like for their ancestors living in slavery. A possible thesis statement that views Dana's journey to the past through a historical lens might be: With *Kindred*, Octavia Butler presents a story that showcases the horrors of slavery, and, in doing so, celebrates the courage and fortitude her ancestors possessed to survive a savage period in US history.

4

OVERVIEWS OF
A WRINKLE IN TIME AND *1984*

Dystopian societies are common themes in science fiction. The word *dystopia* is Greek in origin and translates to "bad place." It is the opposite of the term *utopia*. A dystopia is an unpleasant, nightmarish society.

Both *A Wrinkle in Time* by Madeleine L'Engle and *1984* by George Orwell address the theme of human nature within a dystopian society. *A Wrinkle in Time,* published in 1962, is a coming-of-age story. It carries a political message, warning against the dangers of conformity. It follows Meg Murry, her younger brother Charles Wallace, and a neighbor boy named Calvin O'Keefe as the three children travel through time and space on a mission to rescue Meg's father. The book, which won

Madeline L'Engle later wrote several sequels
to *A Wrinkle in Time*.

the 1963 Newbery Award, features a female protagonist, unusual for science fiction of its time.

Orwell's *1984,* published in 1949, is a story of a man named Winston Smith who lives under a totalitarian

Orwell died in 1950, less than a year after the publication of *1984.*

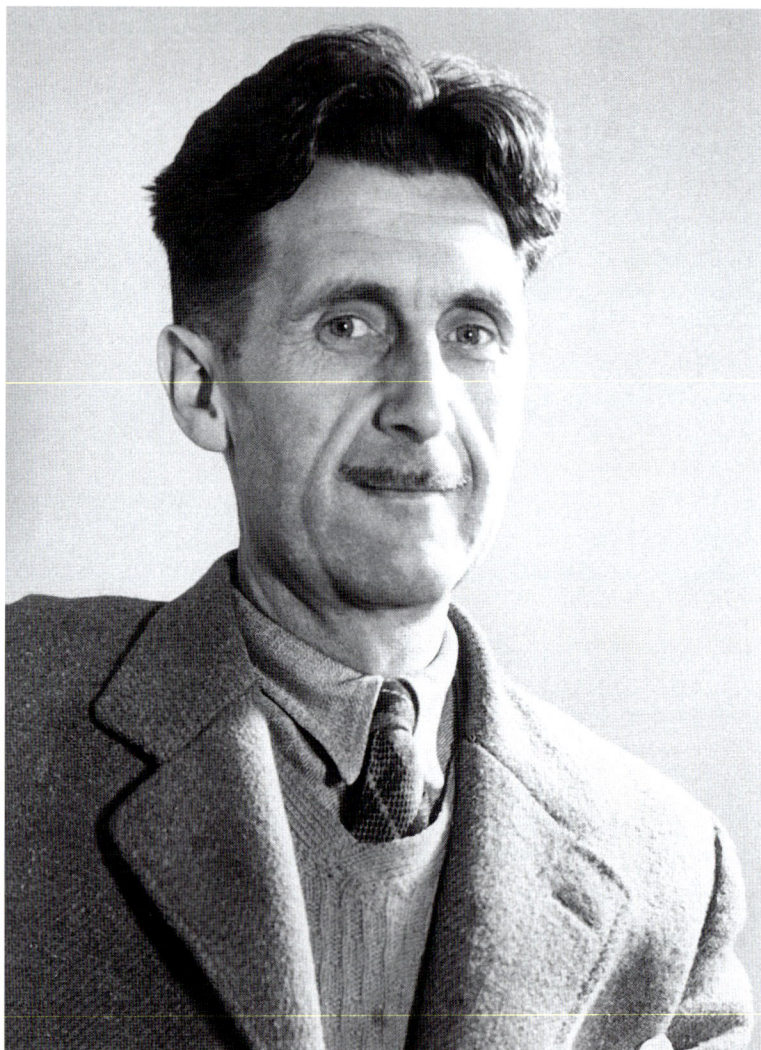

government in which citizens are constantly being watched. Everything they do, say, or even think is scrutinized by the Thought Police. Those who do not fall in line with the Party are not only tortured and killed, but also wiped from history as if they never existed. Both *A Wrinkle in Time* and *1984* present a view of life in a dystopian society and warn against excessive government control of the people.

Not Like the Other Children

Meg Murry is an awkward young teen who struggles to fit in at school. *A Wrinkle in Time* opens with Meg joining her mother and five-year-old brother, Charles Wallace, in the kitchen late at night during a thunderstorm. A boy genius, Charles Wallace speaks like an adult and can seemingly read the minds of his sister and mother. Meg is overly protective of Charles Wallace, which leads her to get into fights at school.

Whereas Meg is plain and insecure, Mrs. Murry is a beautiful, intelligent, confident biologist. Meg's father is a physicist who had been researching the space-time continuum until he mysteriously disappeared a year earlier.

Mrs. Whatsit, Mrs. Who, and Mrs. Which

An eccentric traveler named Mrs. Whatsit comes to the door and meets Meg, her mother, and Charles Wallace. Before she leaves, she startles Mrs. Murry by telling her, "There *is* such a thing as a tesseract."[1] It is evident that Mrs. Whatsit knows something about the missing Mr. Murry. In the story, a tesseract is a fifth dimensional phenomenon that alters space and time as if it were fabric being folded. This allows a person to travel to different points in the space-time continuum without going "the long way around."[2]

The next day, Meg, Charles Wallace, and a neighbor boy named Calvin O'Keefe visit Mrs. Whatsit's cabin in the woods. There, they meet Mrs. Who, who tells them, "The time is not yet ripe. Don't worry, we won't go without you."[3] That night, the children meet up with Mrs. Whatsit, Mrs. Who, and a third strange woman named Mrs. Which. Together, the group is suddenly transported through space to the planet Uriel via a tesseract. It turns out the three women are celestial beings capable of taking on different appearances. They explain their mode of travel is called tessering, or traveling by wrinkling time and hopping from one point to another while skipping a great distance.

The children learn that a great evil called the Black Thing is enveloping planets and threatening the entire universe. Camazotz, the planet on which Mr. Murry is imprisoned, has already fallen to the evil, but the three Mrs. Ws assure Meg and her brother it's not too late to save their father.

Conformity on Camazotz

The group tessers to Camazotz, where the children must proceed alone. They are warned to stay together as they search for Mr. Murry.

Everything on Camazotz appears to be identical, even how the children play. They see a little Camazotz boy bounce his ball out of rhythm. His mother nervously snatches up the boy and rushes indoors with him. The trio learns the planet is run by CENTRAL Central Intelligence, and all citizens must adhere to the Manual, which outlines rules and dictates behavior.

They are brought before a man with red glowing eyes. Charles Wallace allows himself to be hypnotized to help find his father. He becomes a robot-like boy, speaking words that seem to be put into his brain. He tells Meg everyone on Camazotz is much happier because they've learned to give in and submit to IT.

Meg and Calvin fight the forces of conformity to free Meg's father.

Finding Father

The bewitched Charles Wallace shows Meg and Calvin a room. Inside, the little boy they had seen earlier is being tortured and forced to bounce a ball in rhythm. Charles Wallace then leads Meg and Calvin to a transparent column inside which her father is trapped.

Meg is able to free her father from the chamber and the group ends up in front of IT, a large, disembodied, pulsating brain that controls thought on Camazotz. All Camazotzians fall into the rhythm of the pulsating brain. The group is not strong enough to resist IT's ability to infiltrate their thoughts, and just before succumbing to IT's power, Mr. Murry is able to use a tesseract to tesser himself, Meg, and Calvin away to another planet. Charles Wallace is left behind.

Love Prevails

The three Mrs. Ws appear and tell Meg that to save Charles Wallace, she must travel back to Camazotz, this time alone. Mrs. Which tells her just before she is tessered back to Camazotz that she possesses one thing IT does not, but she must discover this weapon for herself.

Meg makes her way past the same identical homes to the CENTRAL Central Intelligence building. There, she comes face to face with the robot Charles Wallace in the presence of IT. It is then that she realizes it's her love for Charles Wallace that is the real weapon. Her sentiment finally reaches through to the real Charles Wallace, and the boy is able to fight his way back from IT's control. The two embrace and are immediately tessered through time and space away from Camazotz and IT.

Meg and Charles Wallace arrive back on Earth. Mr. Murry and Calvin are with them as well. The family is at last reunited, and Mr. and Mrs. Murry run into each other's arms. The three Mrs. Ws appear. Before Mrs. Whatsit can explain why they don't have time for a proper good-bye, the three women are whisked away again on another journey.

1984

The protagonist of *1984* is Winston Smith, a worker in the Records Department in the Ministry of Truth in London in the nation of Oceania. He is a member of the Outer Party, which watches the citizens everywhere they go using screens on the walls and hidden microphones. Citizens can be arrested for anything deemed rebellious, including thinking about rebellion, which is called thoughtcrime. The party's leader is known as Big Brother, and propaganda and posters are placed everywhere to warn and remind people that "Big Brother is Watching You."[4]

Winston's job is to alter historical records according to the Party's wishes. As the story opens, the Party is implementing a new language called Newspeak, which is designed to stifle creative thought, including thoughts about rebellion. The Party believes it can prevent a political rebellion if the citizens aren't allowed to use words relating to it.

Thoughtcrimes

Winston soon becomes frustrated about the rigid control the Party wields over the lives of the people. Winston begins writing his thoughts in a journal in a spot in

The face of Big Brother is a constant presence in the world of *1984*.

his apartment he believes to be out of camera view. At night, he walks through poor neighborhoods in London where the proletarians, or proles, live in poor conditions but seem to be free of surveillance.

One day Winston receives a note from a woman at work named Julia who confesses her love for Winston. The two begin a secret affair, being very careful to stay out of sight of the cameras. Whereas Winston is convinced they'll eventually be caught, Julia is more optimistic. But the more Winston sees Julia, the more he begins to resent the Party. He eventually meets

O'Brien, a man he believes to be a member of the Brotherhood, an anti-Party underground organization. Winston tells O'Brien of his hatred for the totalitarian control by the Party.

After meeting with Winston and questioning him, O'Brien gives Winston a copy of a book supposedly written by the Brotherhood's leader, Emmanuel Goldstein. Winston reads it with Julia in an apartment they have rented in the poor prole district. He then discovers a hidden telescreen just before the Thought Police break in and arrest Julia and him.

The Ministry of Love

The couple is separated and taken to the Ministry of Love, where Winston discovers O'Brien is a Party spy. There, Winston is tortured and brainwashed by O'Brien. Winston initially refuses to accept the concept of "doublethink," the ability to hold two opposing ideas at once. Winston insists the past can't be changed by the Party simply by altering documents. He states that things still exist in human memory and cannot be changed. "Very well, then," replies O'Brien. "We, the Party, control all records, and we control all memories. Then we control the past, do we not?"[5]

After months of brainwashing and torture, Winston is taken to Room 101, the last stop for those accused of crimes against the Party. O'Brien tells Winston he will be faced with his worst fear. O'Brien attaches a cage full of hungry rats to Winston's head, and just before O'Brien opens it to allow the rats to eat Winston's face, Winston snaps, begging them to do it to Julia instead of him.

Defeat

Winston learns it was O'Brien's plan all along to make him break and betray his love for Julia. The Party had been watching Winston for the past seven years and was aware of his thoughtcrimes for a long time.

Winston is finally released, but he is changed. He and Julia see each other, but Winston no longer loves her. She tells him that she, too, betrayed him while being tortured. At the story's end, Winston is sitting at a café. He looks up at the telescreen and thinks to himself his rebelliousness was all a misunderstanding, causing him needless pain. He is glad to finally have "won the victory over himself."[6] In the end, Winston has succumbed to the Party and loves Big Brother.

5

THE BATTLE FOR INDIVIDUALITY

Some forms of criticism draw from external concepts. Historical criticism, drawing from real-world events, is an example of this. A historical critique looks at the historical circumstances of the time in which the work was created. It then analyzes how the work was influenced by this context.

During the 1960s, when *A Wrinkle in Time* was published, the Cold War was underway. This was a period of political and military tension between the United States and the Soviet Union. It began after the nations' alliance in World War II (1939–1945), and

it lasted into the 1990s. A constant threat of nuclear war loomed over both countries as each side viewed the other as an enemy.

Years before, in 1924, Joseph Stalin came into power in Russia. He purged the Communist Party of anyone who didn't agree with him, and he used famine and executions to control the people. The Communist government controlled the press and owned every business. Many Americans viewed the mass conformity that went along with Communism as the death of individuality. Books such as *A Wrinkle in Time* celebrated uniqueness and spoke out against the dangers of too much interference by a controlling power.

George Orwell's *1984* was also written during the Cold War. Published in 1949, the book describes a world of total government surveillance of every aspect of citizens' lives. Although both books address the dangers of totalitarianism, thought control, and censorship, L'Engle's novel lacks the utter despair present throughout *1984*. *A Wrinkle in Time* was written for a younger audience, and at its heart are hope and love. Orwell's *1984*, on the other hand, paints a picture of pure futility. Although both *A Wrinkle in Time* and *1984* illustrate attitudes toward Communism at the time of the Cold War through shared themes, L'Engle's novel suggests conformity can be overthrown by goodness and love, whereas Orwell's novel makes the statement that love and goodness cannot prevail against totalitarianism.

Both novels showcase the fear and paranoia that reign over the citizens in their respective cities. The Camazotzians live in constant fear they will step out of line and be turned in to CENTRAL Central Intelligence. This is evident with the mother who hurries outside to snatch up her son who has mis-bounced his ball.

When Meg, Charles Wallace, and Calvin knock on her door to return the ball, she defensively argues, "Oh no! The children in our section *never* drop balls! They're all perfectly trained. We haven't had an Aberration for

THESIS

Here the author states the thesis: "Although both *A Wrinkle in Time* and *1984* illustrate attitudes toward Communism at the time of the Cold War through shared themes, L'Engle's novel suggests conformity can be overthrown by goodness and love, whereas Orwell's novel makes the statement that love and goodness cannot prevail against totalitarianism."

ARGUMENT ONE

The author makes the first argument, stating a big similarity between the books: "Both novels showcase the fear and paranoia that reign over the citizens in their respective cities."

three years."[1] The mother is clearly extremely afraid of being reported. People avoid stepping out of line on Camazotz out of fear of IT. The reason is clear to Meg and Calvin when they later see the little boy in a room in CI relearning to bounce his ball in perfect cadence as he is being tortured.

Likewise, in *1984*, the citizens of Oceania live in fear of the Party and of breaking the rules. They are under constant surveillance by the authorities through telescreens that are placed in every building, including within their apartments, along with secret microphones and cameras. They hear and read the constant reminder, "Big Brother is Watching You."[2] The Thought Police identify those who are guilty of undermining the Party's regime. If a Party member fails to conform and steps out of line with the doctrines of Big Brother, he or she is "vaporized," tortured and sent to a forced labor camp or killed. The Party makes individual thought even more difficult by encouraging children to report their parents if they suspect potential thoughtcrimes. Orwell demonstrates that under totalitarianism, freedom of thought is not assured even within the home.

Both stories demonstrate the protagonists' strengths come from the fact that they don't fit in and they reject conformity, one of the leading tenets of Communism. At the beginning of *Wrinkle*, Meg is lamenting the fact she is not like the other kids at school. Her principal tries to impress upon her the importance of acting more like the other students. "Try to be a little less antagonistic," he tells her. "Maybe your work would improve if your

ARGUMENT TWO

The author continues to argue the thesis with: "Both stories demonstrate the protagonists' strengths come from the fact that they don't fit in and they reject conformity, one of the leading tenets of Communism."

Conformity in *1984* is seen at massive rallies designed to support the Party.

general attitude were more tractable."[3] The word *tractable* means "easy to control or influence." But it's her uniqueness that gives her the ability to save her father and her brother. She is not docile, like the other girls in her class. She has a temper and spirit, which give her the courage and fortitude to face IT and save her family.

Winston also subverts the conformity that is demanded by the Party. He begins writing a journal criticizing the Party and Big Brother. He falls in love with Julia, which is forbidden, and joins what he believes to be an underground society called the Brotherhood that seeks to destroy the Party. Knowing he could be arrested, tortured, and killed for his thoughtcrimes, Winston is willing to take the risks to fight for his individuality in the Communist-like state. Again, whereas Meg's rejection of conformity gives her the tools needed to save her family, Winston's rebellion ends in torture and reeducation. Ironically, it causes him to love Big Brother even more.

Both novels include systems that control the

ARGUMENT THREE

Here, the author uses argument three to explain a key difference between the books: "Both novels include systems that control the citizens. Meg is able to save her family and escape from this system, whereas Winston's rebellion ends with him succumbing to Big Brother."

citizens. Meg is able to save her family and escape from this system, whereas Winston's rebellion ends with him succumbing to Big Brother. Both Meg and Winston realize the thought control in their respective stories is not freedom. Rather, it is to become a mental zombie to an evil power. But only Meg is successful in rebelling against becoming a mindless follower. When Meg is brought before IT by Charles Wallace, she tries to mentally fight against allowing herself to be controlled by IT. Her father tessers her away before she can be overtaken. However, on her return trip to save her brother, she realizes her love for her brother is stronger than the mind-control IT can try to force upon her. It is this love that finally breaks through to Charles Wallace and saves both of them from the fate of being slaves to the pulsating mind of IT.

Winston, however, is captured by the Thought Police and taken to the Ministry of Love, where he is interrogated and tortured with electroshock. He finally cracks, and under the direction of a Thought Police agent, he confesses to crimes he has not committed. Unlike Meg, Winston betrays Julia, a person he loves. Despite his desperate attempt through the story to fight against the Party, in the end, he loses. Whereas Meg and Charles Wallace are happily reunited, Winston and Julia sever their romantic relationship following their reeducations.

Although both L'Engle and Orwell paint pictures of truly horrific worlds ruled by totalitarian governments that parallel the tenets of Communism, L'Engle's commentary on the nation's social circumstances at the time are presented in a manner that is relatable to a younger audience. Further, though both novels leave no doubt that Communism and conformity bring with them the end of personal freedoms, including the freedom of thought, they do it in dissimilar ways. *A Wrinkle in Time* leaves hope that goodness and love will prevail. *1984* provides a much bleaker outlook on the effects of Communism on a community.

CONCLUSION

In the final paragraph, the author analyzes the final comparison between the two novels, pointing out that although they tackle a similar issue, the final result is very different.

THINKING
CRITICALLY

Consider the following questions:

1. The thesis statement suggests both authors tackle Americans' attitudes toward Communism during the Cold War, yet they both end their stories with a different message. Do you agree with the author's thesis? Why or why not? Would you add anything to it? If so, what?

2. How are the protagonists in *A Wrinkle in Time* and *1984* alike? How are they different?

3. Why do you think L'Engle gave *A Wrinkle in Time* a happy ending? Why do you think Orwell chose to not give *1984* a happy ending?

OTHER
APPROACHES

The critique you have just read is one way to approach *A Wrinkle in Time* through the lens of historical criticism. The following are other ways to apply this approach.

Analyzing the Characters

Whereas Winston grew up within a Communist-like state, Meg is transported to one in her teens. Because of this, their attitudes about their surroundings differ. Meg is keenly aware that things are not as they should be in Camazotz, whereas Winston struggles to remember a time before there was a Big Brother. This leaves room to explore the differences in the characters as they navigate their ways through these environments. A thesis statement for this exploration might be: Through the characters of Meg Murry in *A Wrinkle in Time* and Winston Smith in *1984*, L'Engle and Orwell demonstrate how humans react to life under a totalitarian regime differently, depending on whether they are introduced to it an early age or later in life.

A Wrinkle in Time, 1984, and Feminism

A Wrinkle in Time's Meg is one of the first female protagonists within the science fiction genre. She is a strong-willed young woman who does not conform. In fact, she gets into fights at school defending her brother. In contrast, 1984's Julia is a secondary character to the protagonist, Winston. She is shown as less interested in destroying the Party than Winston, instead seeking only to defy its rules in cases where she has a personal interest. A possible thesis statement for exploring this could be: By portraying the story's heroine as a headstrong, nonconforming teenaged girl, L'Engle is making a pro-feminist statement through her novel A Wrinkle in Time. But in 1984, the female character is relegated to the sidelines, a reflection of the treatment of women within the dystopian world of the novel.

6

AN OVERVIEW OF
THE HITCHHIKER'S GUIDE TO THE GALAXY

The theme of alien life-forms invading Earth with the intent of raiding the planet of its natural resources wasn't new in 1979 when Douglas Adams's *The Hitchhiker's Guide to the Galaxy* debuted. In 1897, H. G. Wells's *War of the Worlds* gave a fictional first-hand account of Martians landing in England to pursue and kill humans and feed off their blood. *War of the Worlds* was one of the earliest alien invasion novels, and it remains one of the most important novels in science fiction history.

Hitchhiker's Guide is a modern, humorous spin on the alien invasion theme. Arthur Dent, an Earthling, awakens one morning in his suburban London, England,

Douglas Adams originally produced *The Hitchhiker's Guide to the Galaxy* as a radio program before adapting it as a novel.

home to find bulldozers waiting to tear down his house to make way for a new bypass. Arthur lies in front of the bulldozer in protest and argues with Mr. Prosser, a local councilman sent to change his mind. Arthur informs Mr. Prosser he was told about the scheduled demolition only the day before, and he comments on the absurdity of the appeal process.

Eventually, Arthur's good friend Ford Prefect appears. After he tells Arthur he is actually from "a small planet somewhere in the vicinity of Betelgeuse," he tells him, "Drink up. The world's about to end."[1]

He informs Arthur the imminent destruction of his home is the least of his worries, as ships from the Vogon Constructor Fleet are ready to destroy the planet Earth to make way for a new hyperspace express bypass. In a direct parallel to Arthur's conversation with Mr. Prosser, humans hear a loud public announcement address from the sky, informing them their planet has been scheduled for demolition. "There's no point in acting all surprised about it," they are told. "All the planning charts and demolition order have been on display in your local planning department in Alpha Centauri for fifty of your Earth years, so you've had plenty of time to lodge any formal complaint and it's far too late to start making a fuss about it now."[2]

Escape

Moments before the Earth is vaporized, Ford, an experienced intergalactic hitchhiker, smuggles himself and Arthur on board a Vogon spacecraft. Hidden on the ship, Ford introduces Arthur to an electronic book called *The Hitchhiker's Guide to the Galaxy*, "the standard

Arthur, *left*, and Ford, *right*, escape the destruction of Earth together.

repository of all knowledge and wisdom."[3] Ford, a researcher and writer for the guide, had arrived on Earth 15 years prior with the intent of staying only one week. He had been waiting for another flying saucer to hitch a ride from ever since.

Still in hiding on the Vogon ship, Ford instructs Arthur to put a small yellow fish in his ear. Just then, an unintelligible voice comes over the ship's public address system. "It's the Vogon captain making an announcement," states Ford.[4] Arthur says he can't understand Vogon, causing Ford to clap his hand to Arthur's ear. The yellow Babel fish slithers down Arthur's ear canal, and soon he can understand every word being said by the alien captain.

Caught

The stowaways are caught and brought before Captain Prostetnic Vogon Jeltz. They are tortured by being forced to listen to Vogon poetry, widely regarded as the worst form of poetry in the galaxy. They are then thrown into an airlock to be cast into space.

"It's at times like this, when I'm trapped in a Vogon airlock with a man from Betelgeuse, and about to die of asphyxiation in deep space, that I really wish I'd listened to what my mother told me when I was young," contemplates Arthur. Ford asks him what his mother had said. "I don't know," he answers. "I didn't listen."[5]

The duo is ejected from the Vogon ship into space. Luckily, before they die, they are picked up by another ship, the *Heart of Gold*. The President of the Imperial Galactic Government, Zaphod Beeblebrox, is at the helm of the stolen ship, which is powered by an Infinite Improbability Drive. Zaphod has a second head and a third arm, which he says helps him immensely with ski-boxing.

In the control room, Zaphod and his companion, Trillian, realize the ship has picked up hitchhikers. They send Marvin, a depressed robot, to fetch the intruders. Meanwhile, Ford explains to Arthur the ship is equipped with GPP, Genuine People Personalities, a feature that allows robots to behave with human personalities. Just then, Marvin enters and the two get a taste of his depressing GPP. On the way to the bridge, Marvin tells the men the ship has been stolen by Zaphod Beeblebrox. Ford is shocked to hear this news.

Ford and Arthur meet Zaphod and Trillian. Ford introduces Zaphod as his "semicousin," but Arthur surprises Ford by telling him the two have already met at a party in England six months prior. Zaphod had interrupted Arthur, who had been talking to a woman at a party, and stole her away. The woman, Tricia McMillan, turns out to be Trillian.

Secrets on Magrathea

Later that night, the crew of four reaches their destination, the planet Magrathea, which had once manufactured new, private planets for the galactic elite. Now, after being inactive for more than 5 million years, the planet's existence has become merely a legend.

The group receives a recorded message from the planet thanking them for their stop but letting them know "the entire planet is temporarily closed for

Zaphod, *center*, and Trillian, *right*, join Arthur and Ford on their adventures.

business."[6] When the ship does not leave, they hear another recorded message, alerting them to nuclear warheads that have been dispatched toward their ship. Although the *Heart of Gold* is unable to take evasive action, Arthur turns on the Improbability Drive, which turns the two missiles into a bowl of petunias and a sperm whale, both of which fall to the ground instead of hitting the ship.

Arthur and Marvin stay with the ship while the others explore Magrathea's underground tunnels. As they explore, Zaphod explains he ran scans on his brains and discovered certain portions had been cauterized. The person who had done it left his initials carved into Zaphod's brain—Z. B. Suddenly, the three collapse from knockout gas.

Meanwhile, Arthur watches the planet's two suns set with Marvin. He begins missing Earth, but he is put off by Marvin's negativity. He goes for a walk and runs into a tall, elderly man with a "thin and distinguished, careworn but not unkind" face, the type "you would happily bank with."[7] The old man, Slartibartfast, tells Arthur the Magratheans are not dead, but have simply been sleeping the last 5 million years until the economy recovers enough that their services of building custom planets are once again in demand. He convinces Arthur to join him, telling him Magrathea was about to awaken.

Slartibartfast takes Arthur to the place where the Magratheans build planets. There, he tells Arthur that they are building a second Earth, just as they had built the first one. He tells Arthur that mice, hyperintelligent beings that can move through dimensions, paid for the first Earth. The mice, Arthur is told, used the planet to conduct one large experiment on humans. Realizing Arthur is confused, Slartibartfast offers to explain the entire story to Arthur.

The story of Earth, according to the old man, started long ago. A species of hyperintelligent beings sought to find the meaning of life. They built a giant supercomputer named Deep Thought. But when the programmers turned it on, the computer announced it would be surpassed by a more powerful computer, and then two philosophers demanded the supercomputer could not work on solving the meaning of life. According to them, only philosophers should sit up all night debating whether there is or is not a god. "We demand rigidly defined areas of doubt and uncertainty!" shouted Philosopher Vroomfondel.[8] Deep Thought reassured the philosophers it would take it 7.5 million years to compute the correct answer, so their jobs were safe, at least for a little while.

Slartibartfast provides Arthur with Sens-O-Tape recordings of what happened after the 7.5 million years. As a huge audience awaited the answer, two computer programmers were ready for Deep Thought to relay life's biggest mystery. But the computer warned they wouldn't like the answer before he divulged, "The Answer to the Great Question of Life, the Universe and Everything . . . is . . . 42!"[9]

After much confusion, the computer programmers asked Deep Thought what question 42 is the answer for. What is the Great Question, they wanted to know. Deep Thought explained that only a much more complex computer, which would come later, could answer that question. That computer was Earth.

The Mice

Ford, Zaphod, and Trillian awake to discover they are in a catalog of custom planets. The three discuss the situation with Zaphod's brain. He figures he sealed off part of his brain so no one would know something he knew, but he couldn't remember what. He does recall that a man named Yooden Vranx convinced Zaphod to steal the *Heart of Gold* just before he died. He also warned Zaphod to hide the reasons he was stealing it, or it would show up on brain scans before he was elected president. A Magrathean man appears and announces, "The mice will see you now."[10]

Slartibartfast sums up his story with Arthur: "Deep Thought designed the Earth, we built it and you lived on it."[11] After telling Arthur about some plans for Earth Two, he tells the man the mice are ready to meet him.

Arthur is reunited with Ford, Zaphod, and Trillian, who are eating a big meal. They introduce him to two mice, Frankie and Benjy, whom Trillian brought with her from Earth. The mice inform Slartibartfast they won't need another Earth after all. Instead, they would like to dissect Arthur's brain to see whether the Great Question is hidden deep inside. They figure that because he was on Earth up until the very last moment of its existence, his brain, an organic part of the computer matrix, might contain information. They offer to replace his brain with a simple electronic one. Arthur declines their offer, but the mice reply menacingly that it's not negotiable. Arthur, Ford, Zaphod, and Trillian narrowly escape the mice, some Magrathean thugs, and policemen who have come to arrest Zaphod for

theft. That night on the ship, Arthur decides that he'd better acquaint himself with the *Guide,* because he is stuck in this place. He reads an article that explains all civilizations go through three stages: Survival, Inquiry, and Sophistication.

He reads, "For instance, the first phase is characterized by the question *How can we eat?* the second by the question *Why do we eat?* and the third by the question *Where shall we go have lunch?*"[12] Just then, Zaphod comes over the intercom and asks Arthur if he is hungry. When Arthur says he could eat, Zaphod replies they'll stop at the Restaurant at the End of the Universe.

FUNNY SOCIAL COMMENTARY AND THE END OF THE WORLD

Social commentary is the act of expressing an opinion on the nature of society, often with the intent to help promote change. Social commentators regularly express their opinions about topics such as politics, education, society, and the environment. Social commentators aim to educate and inform the general public about a social issue with the goal of appealing to people's sense of justice.

Some social commentators are outspoken and blunt. These often include hosts of political programs or television talk shows. They may argue with their opponents to demand change. But others offer opinions

Adams uses the characters of *The Hitchhiker's Guide to the Galaxy* to convey social commentary mixed with humor.

on social issues in a more subtle way. Some do it through music or artwork. Others present social issues for the public's consideration through writing.

Douglas Adams's *The Hitchhiker's Guide to the Galaxy* is a humorous novel that tells the story of Arthur Dent, a space-traveling refugee from the demolished planet Earth. Adams creates a fun cast of characters with entertaining backstories and funny dialogue. On the surface, it is a lighthearted science fiction story with themes that are still relevant today. However, Adams presents several situations that illustrate real-world problems in society. Through the use of satirical and humorous social commentary, Adams sends strong messages about the ridiculous nature of many parts of modern life.

One of the tools Adams employs is the use of an outsider's perspective to point out some of the flaws with humankind. The narrator of the book, an unnamed observer with a third-person perspective, starts off the story by commenting on the general state of humankind:

> *This planet has—or had—a problem, which was this: most of the people living on it were unhappy for pretty much of the time. Many solutions were suggested for this problem, but most of these were largely concerned with the movements of small green pieces of paper, which is odd because on the whole it wasn't the small green pieces of paper that were unhappy.[1]*

Adams points out society's obsession with money and the ultimate unhappiness of most people in operating within the monetary system. The author is stating money does not bring happiness. Instead, the constant focus on moving around "small green pieces of paper" is absurd and only leads to misery. He goes on to write, "And so the problem remained; lots of the people were mean, and most of them were miserable."[2] Adams suggests that, through a humorous presentation of the facts, the majority could have pursued other solutions rather than remaining fixated on money, but those people chose not to explore those options.

Another way in which Adams comments on social issues is by pointing out the ridiculous and often futile ways that people are forced to navigate society's complex, seemingly arbitrary rules. As his house is about to be demolished, Arthur tells Mr. Prosser, "The first I knew about it was when a workman arrived at my home yesterday."[3] Mr. Prosser replies the plans were on display for months, suggesting Arthur had ample time to take appropriate steps to appeal the demolition of his home. But, like many situations in society, especially those involving government bureaucracies, the rules are so complicated and obscure the average person has little to no hope of success. Arthur shares that he eventually found the plans, "on display in the bottom of a locked filing cabinet stuck in a disused lavatory with a sign on the door saying 'Beware of the Leopard.'"[4] Adams's humorous explanation of Arthur's attempts to find the plans illustrates how futile it would have been for Arthur to try halting the demolition.

Adams draws a further illustration of preposterous protocol when Ford convinces Mr. Prosser to lie down in the mud and take Arthur's place blocking the bulldozer, allowing Ford and Arthur to leave and visit a pub. Ford's logic is that because everyone could assume Arthur would lie there all day, it is not necessary for him to actually do so, as long as everyone accepts that those are his intentions. Having Mr. Prosser take his place in the mud is unnecessary, yet to follow through with this logic, someone has to block the bulldozer—even if it's

Adams uses the science fiction elements of the story, such as the spaceship *Heart of Gold,* to satirize modern life.

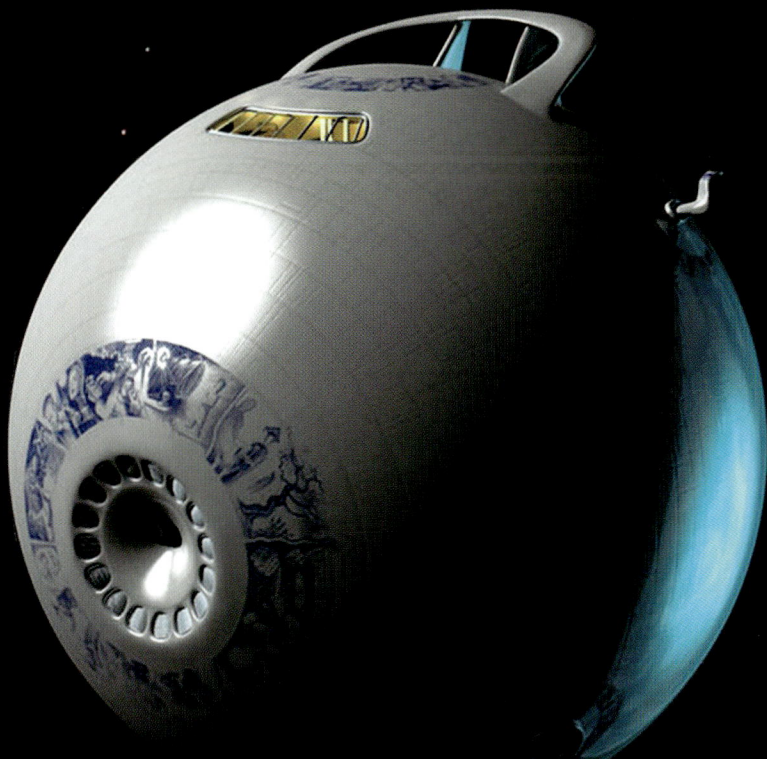

ARGUMENT THREE

The author next tackles the subject of politics as it is presented in *A Hitchhiker's Guide to the Galaxy*: "Adams satirizes the galaxy's government to show not only the corruption of politics, but also the vast social ignorance of how government structure actually works."

the person who intends to use the bulldozer.

Adams satirizes the galaxy's government to show not only the corruption of politics, but also the vast social ignorance of how government structure actually works. Zaphod Beeblebrox may hold the prestigious title of President of the Imperial Galactic Government, but the narrator notes, "Only six people in the entire Galaxy understood the principle on which the Galaxy was governed."[5] The author inserts a comical footnote explaining:

> The President in particular is very much a figurehead—he wields no real power whatsoever. He is apparently chosen by the government, but the qualities he is required to display are not those of leadership but those of finely judged outrage. For this reason the President is always a controversial choice, always an infuriating but fascinating character. His job is not to wield power but to draw attention away from it.[6]

Although the book was published in 1979, the social message still holds true today. Corruption is possible when people fail to pay attention to what politicians are actually doing. The fact that only six people truly understand the system of government speaks to the ignorance of those being governed.

Adams continues his social commentary on modern bureaucracy by explaining the President is merely a figurehead, and an entertaining one at that. Adams specifically states it was Zaphod's job to distract the people by drawing attention away from those who hold the real power and make the decisions. Adams is commenting on how the majority of people are more concerned with looks and personalities during an election rather than actual credentials. Further, after electing a president, many people are far more interested in tabloid stories involving leaders and politicians than they are about current events and how those leaders are addressing them. The indifference with which many approach accountability in political leaders is mirrored when Adams states, "Most of the others secretly believe that the ultimate decision-making process is handled by a computer. They couldn't be more wrong."[7]

The Hitchhiker's Guide to the Galaxy appears, on the surface, to be a fun, comical, science fiction romp through the galaxy. But the book is filled with instances where author Douglas Adams humorously points out the shortcomings of society. His social commentary draws to the surface several themes, including unhappiness, greed, modern-day politics, and the meaning of life. He suggests, among other things, that humankind should consider shifting focus from things such as money to more important things, such as holding political leaders accountable for their actions.

CONCLUSION

The author wraps up the arguments and ties them back to the original thesis.

THINKING
CRITICALLY

Now it's your turn to assess the essay. Consider these questions:

1. Do you agree with the thesis? Why or why not?

2. How could one make the argument that Douglas Adams's *The Hitchhiker's Guide to the Galaxy* does not contain social commentary?

3. A conclusion should restate the thesis and main arguments. Are there any sentences in the conclusion that could be removed or simplified? Remove or modify one sentence and explain your reasoning.

OTHER
APPROACHES

What you have read is one possible way to critique *The Hitchhiker's Guide to the Galaxy*. The following are two other approaches.

British Humor

Douglas Adams was a British man who was highly influenced by popular British comedy. Before writing *Hitchhiker's Guide*, he wrote for the popular British comedy show *Monty Python's Flying Circus*. One of the hallmarks of British humor is absurdity. This is evident with Adams's writing, particularly when Arthur and Ford are about to be expelled from the Vogon spaceship and are facing imminent death by suffocation. During a very serious time, Arthur and Ford still exchange absurd humor while they await the opening of the airlock. A possible thesis statement for a critique that explores the use of humor might be: The use of absurd British humor throughout *The Hitchhiker's Guide to the Galaxy* creates a lighthearted plot in a book that tackles otherwise serious societal issues involving genocide, politics, religion, the meaning of life, and many others.

A Lack of Female Characters

Of all the characters in the book, there is only one notable woman, Trillian. Her part is very limited. During the 1960s, feminists in the United States began fighting for equality for women. This second-wave feminism, as it was called, eventually spread to Europe and other parts of the world by the early 1980s. How might Adams have written his story differently ten years later, after Europe experienced this second-wave feminist activism? A critique that explores this question might have the thesis statement: The Hitchhiker's Guide to the Galaxy serves as an example of pre–second-wave-feminist literature due to its glaring lack of female characters.

8

AN OVERVIEW OF
THE 5TH WAVE

The 5th Wave is an alien invasion science fiction novel written by Rick Yancey. It tells the story of Cassie Sullivan, a 16-year-old girl from Ohio who is trying to save her little brother, Sammy, from an alien-run military compound. The Others, as the aliens are called in the book, look and sound exactly like humans. Their plan is to annihilate the human race and inhabit the planet. Cassie travels to retrieve Sammy while trying to stay alive and tell friend from foe.

The Waves

The arrival of the Others is followed by waves of destruction. The 1st Wave is an electro-magnetic pulse (EMP), a surge of energy that disables objects and machinery that use electricity, including vehicles. More

Author Rick Yancey also wrote two sequels to *The 5th Wave*.

than half a million people die when cars suddenly crash and planes fall out of the sky.

The 2nd Wave kills 3 billion people. The Others drop enormous rods, each twice as tall as the Empire State Building, onto Earth's fault lines. The resulting earthquakes cause tsunamis that wipe out the coastlines, where 40 percent of the planet's population lives.

The 3rd Wave is a deadly virus that is carried by birds and transmitted via bird excrement. Victims bleed to death. The virus claims 97 percent of all remaining humans, including Cassie's mother. In the wake of the 3rd Wave, cities and towns are littered with dead bodies. With no plumbing, no electricity, and limited supplies, the remaining humans are left to battle for survival.

Following the death of Cassie's mother, her father decides it is not safe for them to stay in their home. He packs up his children and the three set out on a journey to Wright-Patterson Air Force Base in Ohio, where Cassie's father believes they'll find help and protection. Along the way, they come to a refugee camp, Camp Ashpit. It's here that Cassie comes face to face with the 4th Wave. A military battalion arrives, led by Colonel Vosch. Believing they have been saved, Cassie soon

Cassie struggles to survive a series of deadly events triggered by attacking aliens.

discovers the military personnel are human hosts with an alien consciousness who are intent on destroying the remaining survivors. This is the 4th Wave—assassins she calls Silencers who look human but are not. The children, Sammy included, are rounded up and sent by bus to Camp Haven, a training facility. The adults are assembled and killed. Cassie watches Colonel Vosch shoot and kill her father as she narrowly escapes.

Trust No One

Armed with guns and carrying Sammy's teddy bear, Cassie makes her way toward Camp Haven on foot. "The first rule of surviving the 4th Wave is don't trust anyone," she relates.[1] "The only way to stay alive is to stay alone. That's rule number two."[2]

Meanwhile, Sammy and the other children arrive at Camp Haven. There, children as young as five years old are convinced aliens have taken over human bodies and they must fight as the resistance. The children are unaware the military personnel there are actually the Others. These children become the 5th Wave, an army of children trained to fight and kill any remaining humans.

At Camp Haven, Sammy is given the name Nugget and is assigned to Squad 53. He meets Ben Parish, a boy Cassie had gone to school with and had a crush on. Ben had been brought to Camp Haven sick with the virus. He was healed by a woman named Dr. Pam and then put through a program known as Wonderland, during which he was pressured into killing a boy he was told was infected with an alien. Now known as Private Zombie, Ben becomes friends with Sammy and treats him like a younger brother. Some of the other members of Squad 53 include Ringer, Teacup, Poundcake, Flintstone, and Oompa. Ringer, a girl, is the best shot in the group. She befriends Ben and teaches him how to shoot.

Help from a Stranger

As Cassie makes her way along the Ohio freeway, she is shot in the knee by a Silencer and scrambles under a car for protection. There, she passes out. She awakens in a bed in a farmhouse, her leg bandaged. She meets her savior, Evan Walker. He has lost his entire family. Evan, a handsome, tall, muscular 19-year-old, spends the next few weeks nursing her back to health. The two become close, and Evan eventually kisses her.

When Cassie is well enough to walk, she insists on pushing onward toward her brother. Evan, who has fallen for Cassie, will not allow her to go alone. Cassie doesn't completely trust Evan, but realizes she could use his help. As they make their way toward Camp Haven, Cassie suspects Evan might be an Other. After he takes down a group of juvenile Silencers who attack them, he finally confirms her suspicion, admitting he is also a Silencer and was the one who shot her. He explains to her why he was unable to finish the job, telling her, "Because I'm in love with you."[3]

Cassie struggles with learning Evan is an Other, but he convinces her he doesn't mean her any harm. The two decide to proceed with shutting down Camp Haven and rescuing Sammy.

Resistance

Ben and Sammy continue to train with the army, believing real humans are actually infected with Others. Squad 53 is sent on its first mission. While they are out, Ben and Ringer realize they have been deceived. Upon processing, all the children were implanted with tracking chips. Ben and Ringer find out the chips are, in fact, devices that can kill the child immediately. It becomes clear to them they are being used to kill their fellow human beings.

Ben and Ringer devise a plan to rescue Sammy, who remains back at the base. Ben has Ringer shoot him to cause a minor injury. Ben calls for help, claiming he was shot during the mission, and he is airlifted back to base. After he is treated, Vosch tells him he will be put through the Wonderland program.

Cassie is able to board a bus and arrives on base. Dr. Pam calls her in for processing, but Cassie is able to knock the doctor unconscious. She then sets out to find her brother. Ben also escapes and steals a uniform. Cassie eventually finds Sammy after having to kill an officer who tries to stop her. Just then, Ben arrives. Cassie realizes Ben has not been brainwashed. Sammy tells her his new name is Nugget, and that Ben is now called Zombie. Cassie holds Sammy as Ben cuts his tracker out.

The three agree to leave together, but Colonel Vosch captures them all. He separates them and takes Ben and Cassie to the room where Ben was forced to kill the boy. "Do you know why we will win this war?" taunts Vosch. "Because we know how you think. We've been watching you for six thousand years."[4] He then shows them Sammy, strapped to a chair with electrodes attached to his head. Vosch tells Cassie the only way he will spare Sammy is if she tells him who helped her infiltrate the base. When Cassie insists she was working alone, Vosch hits the button to electrocute Sammy. Although the boy is hurt, he is alive. Vosch realizes Evan has hacked into the base's computers and storms out of the room.

Cassie and Ben are able to overpower the Silencers left to guard them. They are joined by Evan, who says good-bye as he leaves to set off bombs throughout the base. Cassie, Sammy, and Ben are joined by other members of Squad 53. They escape in a Humvee, riding off as bombs destroy the base.

9

ARCHETYPAL CRITICISM OF *THE 5TH WAVE*

Archetypal criticism evaluates a book, film, or other piece of art through archetypes, commonly recurring symbols in real life or in literature. A reader or a viewer can readily relate to these frequently used themes. Swiss psychiatrist Carl Jung developed the idea of archetypes in the 1910s. He made famous the notion that people share a collective unconscious that allows them to recognize familiar characters or situations. Working in the 1940s, US writer Joseph Campbell

Cassie is the hero of the story, but she also takes on other archetypal roles as the narrative progresses.

expanded Jung's ideas, recognizing similar narrative patterns in literary works around the world.

Some familiar archetypal characters are the hero, the damsel in distress, the underdog, the mother and father figures, and the mentor. Archetypes are not limited to characters. They can also include concepts and ideas. The reader or the viewer finds these archetypes familiar and can connect with these people or ideas, causing them to share emotionally in the experiences.

One common theme in science fiction is the setting of a postapocalyptic wasteland, in which a small number of people struggle to survive in a world laid waste by natural forces or invasion. In the early 2000s, this trend became popular in young adult novels. Examples include *The Hunger Games*, *The Maze Runner*, and *Divergent*. In these series, teenagers are forced to fight to save what's left of humanity because the adults are unable to do so. The protagonists eventually take on the role of hero. Although *The 5th Wave* presents many of the typical archetypes found in

THESIS

The author states the thesis. The following arguments will provide evidence to support it: "Although *The 5th Wave* presents many of the typical archetypes found in postapocalyptic literature, the story challenges the usual characteristics of these archetypes and assigns multiple archetypal roles to some of its main characters."

postapocalyptic literature, the story challenges the usual characteristics of these archetypes and assigns multiple archetypal roles to some of its main characters.

Cassie, the book's protagonist, is established as a girl on a coming-of-age quest, but later adds the archetypes of damsel in distress and mother figure. The quest theme has been a common archetype in literature dating back thousands of years. One very famous character on a quest was Odysseus in Homer's ancient epic tale *The Odyssey,* written in the 700s BCE. Often, the person on the quest is a hero who has to undergo several hardships or trials to achieve a goal. Although Cassie endures numerous physical and emotional hardships, she subverts the common hero on a quest archetype when she becomes the damsel in distress for a significant amount of time. Evan saves her and nurses her back to health. Weak and at his mercy, she begins to fall for her handsome savior, a common response for the damsel in distress character. She has not forgotten her task of

ARGUMENT ONE

The author begins to argue the thesis by noting the shift in archetype of the story's protagonist: "Cassie, the book's protagonist, is established as a girl on a coming-of-age quest, but later adds the archetypes of damsel in distress and mother figure."

finding her brother, but she is distracted as her feelings for Evan grow.

Cassie further subverts the modern quest archetype by the fact that by the end of the book, she has neither saved mankind nor caused the downfall of the Others. Unlike other heroic characters, such as Harry Potter or Frodo Baggins of the Lord of the Rings series, Cassie is not the chosen one who will personally save humanity from evil forces. She successfully gets her brother back, but it is Evan who destroys Camp Haven.

Cassie takes on the role of mother early on in the story, before her mother dies. As her father tends to her sick and dying mother, Cassie is left to care for Sammy, and she takes her role seriously. "We'd gotten pretty tight since Mom got sick," Cassie says. "Nearly every night bad dreams chased him into my room, and he'd crawl in bed with me and press his face against my chest, and sometimes he forgot and called me Mommy."[1] She goes on to explain that as she's lying under a car bleeding after being shot, "Sammy is the reason I didn't give up."[2] Cassie talks about caring for Sammy when they were in Camp Ashpit, going through actions a mother would do with her child, such as tucking him in and saying his prayers with him. The ultimate example of how Cassie takes on the mother archetype is the way in which she does not give up, even when shot, to soldier onward and save Sammy. Despite Evan's insistence that heading into Camp Haven is suicide, she refuses to write off her little brother, in just the same way a mother would willingly sacrifice herself to save her child.

Good-looking Evan Walker appears to fit with the knight in shining armor archetype, but Cassie learns in time that although he saved her, he is the enemy. Evan, the good-looking, all-American farm boy from Ohio, comes to Cassie's rescue when she is shot and bleeding to death on the highway. He tends to her wounds, administers medication, bathes her, and helps to rehabilitate her. Without him coming to her rescue as the knight archetype, Cassie would have died of her gunshot wound. But, in a twist, Cassie learns Evan was the one who shot her in the first place. This subverts the typical theme of the knight saving a damsel in distress.

ARGUMENT TWO

Here the author points out the nontraditional archetypal nature of the character of Evan: "Good-looking Evan Walker appears to fit with the knight in shining armor archetype, but Cassie learns in time that although he saved her, he is the enemy."

Evan is seen as both an enemy and a hero in the story.

Evan goes beyond the typical role of knight and love interest when he becomes the enemy. He is lost between two worlds: his humanity and his alien consciousness. He shares with Cassie the plans of his fellow aliens, the Others, but then explains he did not agree with them. He tells Cassie, "There were some of us who didn't think annihilation was the answer. I was one of them, Cassie. My side lost the argument."[3] Cassie struggles with whether to trust him. He has gone from her savior to her love interest to the enemy.

Ultimately, Cassie is left to see Evan in the role of hero. He puts himself in great danger to accompany her to Camp Haven in order to save Sammy. Evan's fate is left uncertain at the end of the book. He says his good-byes to Cassie and then leaves to set off bombs, ensuring the escape of Cassie, Sammy, Ben, and the rest of Squad 53.

Ben Parish, also known as Zombie, seems to symbolize the jock archetype, but he subverts the archetype by taking on the father archetype for Sammy's sake. At the story's outset, Cassie shares that she has a crush on Ben, or as she calls him, "Ben You-Were-Some-Kind-of-Serious-Gorgeous Parish," but continues to explain, "He barely knew I existed. I knew some of the same people he knew, but I was a girl in the background, several degrees of separation removed."[4] Ben is described as being a star football player, and he admits to having a healthy ego to go with his jock status. "I gave her my best smile," he says of his squad mate Ringer. "Before the alien Armageddon happened, I was known for my smile. Not bragging too much, but I had to be careful never to smile while I drove: It had the capacity to blind oncoming traffic."[5]

Despite his good looks and popularity, at Camp Haven Ben finds a soft spot in his heart for Sammy and

ARGUMENT THREE

The final argument takes a look at another male character in the story: "Ben Parish, also known as Zombie, seems to symbolize the jock archetype, but he subverts the archetype by taking on the father archetype for Sammy's sake."

does what he can to protect the boy. He even returns alone to Camp Haven to save Sammy after he and Ringer discover the truth about the tracking devices. His change in character shifts him from someone who is so adored at school that he does not even notice Cassie to a self-sacrificing father figure for a young boy.

The 5th Wave succeeds in presenting postapocalyptic literature in a new light. The author alters common archetypes, stereotypes, and tropes. Cassie is quester, damsel in distress, and mother. Evan's journey sees him through the different archetypes of knight in shining armor, enemy, and hero. And Ben evolves from the athletic jock who thinks highly of himself to a father figure willing to walk into the enemy's lair in order to save a helpless boy. The novel contains a cast of characters who do not fit into the neatly assigned archetype roles that are familiar to readers.

CONCLUSION

In the final paragraph, the author points out that *The 5th Wave* may be a classic postapocalyptic science fiction story, but it subverts the normal ways in which archetypes are assigned.

THINKING
CRITICALLY

Now it's your turn to assess the essay. Consider these questions:

1. *The 5th Wave* takes place in a postapocalypse world. Do you think the setting affects the archetypes and the characters' behaviors? If so, how?

2. Consider the arguments the author has made about Cassie. What additional evidence from the book could support the author's claims? Is there evidence that contradicts the author's thesis?

3. *The 5th Wave* includes archetypes typical of a quest story. In what ways is *The 5th Wave* a classic quest? In what ways is it unique or different?

OTHER

APPROACHES

The critique you have just read is one way to approach *The 5th Wave* through the lens of archetypal criticism. The following are other ways to apply this approach.

The Quest

The 5th Wave is in many ways an example of quest literature. Cassie's ultimate goal is to find and save her brother. She has many miles to travel on foot to reach Camp Haven, where her brother is being kept. Along the way, she must deal with Silencers, as well as other human survivors that might mean her harm. She must overcome her gunshot wound and press on to reach Sammy. She is forced to attack Dr. Pam to gain freedom to search for her brother. By the end of the book, she emerges victorious in her quest when she frees Sammy and the two ride off with the rest of Squad 53. A possible thesis for this argument might be: *The 5th Wave* modernizes the archetypal theme of the quest by presenting the hero as a determined but naïve young girl, rifle slung over her shoulder and teddy bear tucked under her arm.

Lack of a Mentor

Often with quest literature, the hero is able to complete the journey with the help of a mentor or guide. This is usually someone who imparts critical knowledge to the protagonist. One example is what Yoda does for Luke Skywalker in the Star Wars films. Although Cassie has her father throughout the first three waves, he is killed during the 4th Wave, leaving her alone to journey to Camp Haven to get Sammy. It could be argued that Cassie's journey begins with the death of her father. With Mr. Sullivan gone, Cassie is the only one left to save Sammy. How is her quest affected by the fact that she is in a world where the only way to remain safe is to stay alone? What are the consequences of her limited knowledge?

A thesis about the lack of a mentor for Cassie could be: Cassie's quest differs from the usual archetypal quest due to the isolation of the postapocalyptic world. Her lack of a mentor forces her to rely more heavily on her own intuition, ultimately leading her to the truth about Evan.

ANALYZE IT!

Now that you have learned different approaches to analyzing a work, are you ready to perform your own analysis? You have read that this type of evaluation can help you look at literature in a new way and make you pay attention to certain issues you may not have otherwise recognized. So, why not use one of these approaches to consider a fresh take on your favorite work?

First, choose a philosophy, critical theory, or other approach and consider which work or works you want to analyze. Remember the approach you choose is a springboard for asking questions about the works.

Next, write a specific question that relates to your approach or philosophy. Then you can form your thesis, which should provide the answer to that question. Your thesis is the most important part of your analysis and offers an argument about the work, considering its characters, plot, or literary techniques, or what it says about society or the world. Recall that the thesis statement typically appears at the very end of the introductory paragraph of your essay. It is usually only one sentence long.

After you have written your thesis, find evidence to back it up. Good places to start are in the work itself or in journals or articles that discuss what other people have said about it. You may also want to read about the author or creator's life so you can get a sense of what factors may have affected the creative process. This can be especially useful if you are considering how the work connects to history or the author's intent.

You should also explore parts of the book that seem to disprove your thesis and create an argument against them. As you do this, you might want to address what others have written about the book. Their quotes may help support your claim.

Before you start analyzing a work, think about the different arguments made in this book. Reflect on how evidence supporting the thesis was presented. Did you find that some of the techniques used to back up the arguments were more convincing than others? Try these methods as you prove your thesis in your own analysis paper.

When you are finished writing your analysis, read it over carefully. Is your thesis statement understandable? Do the supporting arguments flow logically, with the topic of each paragraph clearly stated? Can you add any information that would present your readers with a stronger argument in favor of your thesis? Were you able to use quotes from the book, as well as from other critics, to enhance your ideas?

Did you see the work in a new light?

GLOSSARY

ABERRATION
Something that is out of the normal expectation.

ASPHYXIATION
To cause to stop breathing, usually resulting in death.

BUREAUCRACY
The body of officials and administrators of a government.

CAUTERIZE
To burn tissue to stop bleeding or destroy infection.

CELESTIAL
Of or relating to the sky and visible heavenly bodies.

CENSORSHIP
The act of imposing values on others by limiting what they may read, write, hear, or see.

DOCTRINE
What is taught; teachings.

FUGITIVE
A person who runs away to avoid recapture.

INFRACTION
An action that breaks a rule or law.

INTERGALACTIC
Occurring between two or more galaxies.

MALARIA
A disease that is spread to humans through mosquito bites.

MATRIX

A collection of circuit elements that perform a particular function.

PHENOMENON

An observed event, especially one with an unclear or unknown explanation.

PHYSICIST

A scientist who studies physics, which deals with matter and energy.

PROLETARIAN

A person belonging to the working class of society.

PROPAGANDA

Information that carries facts or details slanted to favor a single point of view or political bias.

PROTAGONIST

The main character in a book, movie, play, poem, or other work.

RACISM

Poor treatment of or violence against people because of their race.

RUDIMENTARY

Basic or simple.

SATIRIZE

To use humor to point out bad or foolish qualities.

SPACE-TIME CONTINUUM

A four-dimensional continuum that includes length, width, height, and time.

THEME

The subject or main idea of a creative work.

TOTALITARIANISM

A political concept that subjects citizens to total control by an autocratic authority.

TROPE

A common theme or literary technique.

ADDITIONAL
RESOURCES

SELECTED BIBLIOGRAPHY

Adams, Douglas. *The Hitchhiker's Guide to the Galaxy.* New York: Random, 2005. Print.

Butler, Octavia E. *Kindred.* Boston: Beacon, 1979. Print.

L'Engle, Madeleine. *A Wrinkle in Time.* New York: Crosswicks, 1962. Print.

Orwell, George. *1984.* New York: Harcourt, 1949. Print.

Yancey, Rick. *The 5th Wave.* New York: Penguin, 2013. Print.

FURTHER READINGS

Bould, Mark, ed. *The Routledge Companion to Science Fiction.* New York: Routledge, 2009. Print.

Hamen, Susan. *How to Analyze the Films of James Cameron.* Minneapolis, MN: Abdo, 2012. Print.

Seed, David. *Science Fiction: A Very Short Introduction.* Oxford, United Kingdom: Oxford, 2011. Print.

WEBSITES

To learn more about Essential Literary Genres, visit **booklinks.abdopublishing.com**. These links are routinely monitored and updated to provide the most current information available.

FOR MORE INFORMATION

For more information on this subject, contact or visit the following organizations:

Comic-Con

San Diego Convention Center
111 West Harbor Drive
San Diego, CA 92101
http://www.comic-con.org
This annual comic book convention has evolved into the most popular gathering of comic book, science fiction, and fantasy fans in the nation. Each year, it is held in San Diego, California, and is attended by more than 100,000 fans, many dressed in costumes.

EMP Museum at Seattle Center

Science Fiction and Fantasy Hall of Fame
325 5th Avenue North
Seattle, WA 98109
206-770-2700
http://www.empmuseum.org
Founded in 1996, the Science Fiction and Fantasy Hall of Fame is located at the EMP Museum in Seattle, Washington. Hall of Fame inductees are chosen by a panel of award-winning science fiction and fantasy authors, editors, artists, and others, and are then voted upon by the public.

SOURCE NOTES

CHAPTER 1. INTRODUCTION TO LITERARY GENRES

None.

CHAPTER 2. AN OVERVIEW OF *KINDRED*

1. Octavia Butler. *Kindred.* Boston: Beacon, 1979. Print. 13.
2. Ibid. 65.
3. Ibid. 74.
4. Ibid. 95.
5. Ibid. 131.
6. Ibid. 257.

CHAPTER 3. TIME TRAVEL AND THE FIGHT FOR RACIAL EQUALITY

1. Octavia Butler. *Kindred.* Boston: Beacon, 1979. Print. 175.
2. Ibid. 177.
3. Ibid. 178.
4. Ibid.
5. Ibid. 95.

CHAPTER 4. OVERVIEWS OF *A WRINKLE IN TIME* AND *1984*

1. Madeleine L'Engle. *A Wrinkle in Time.* New York: Crosswicks, 1962. Print. 27.
2. Ibid. 88.
3. Ibid. 43.
4. George Orwell. *1984.* New York: Harcourt, 1949. Print. 2.
5. Ibid. 248.
6. Ibid. 298.

CHAPTER 5. THE BATTLE FOR INDIVIDUALITY

1. Madeleine L'Engle. *A Wrinkle in Time.* New York: Macmillan, 1962. Print. 117.
2. George Orwell. *1984.* New York: Harcourt, 1949. Print. 2.
3. Madeleine L'Engle. *A Wrinkle in Time.* New York: Macmillan, 1962. Print. 33.

CHAPTER 6. AN OVERVIEW OF *THE HITCHHIKER'S GUIDE TO THE GALAXY*

1. Douglas Adams. *The Hitchhiker's Guide to the Galaxy.* New York: Random, 2005. Print. 23.
2. Ibid. 35.
3. Ibid. 3.
4. Ibid. 56.
5. Ibid. 75.
6. Ibid. 124.
7. Ibid. 151.
8. Ibid. 172.
9. Ibid. 180–181.
10. Ibid. 191.
11. Ibid. 192.
12. Ibid. 215.

CHAPTER 7. FUNNY SOCIAL COMMENTARY AND THE END OF THE WORLD

1. Douglas Adams. *The Hitchhiker's Guide to the Galaxy.* New York: Random, 2005. Print. 1.
2. Ibid.
3. Ibid. 9.
4. Ibid. 9.
5. Ibid. 37–38.
6. Ibid. 38.
7. Ibid. 38.

CHAPTER 8. AN OVERVIEW OF *THE 5TH WAVE*

1. Rick Yancey. *The 5th Wave.* New York: Speak, 2013. Print. 8.
2. Ibid. 9.
3. Ibid. 362.
4. Ibid. 435.

CHAPTER 9. ARCHETYPAL CRITICISM OF *THE 5TH WAVE*

1. Rick Yancey. *The 5th Wave.* New York: Speak, 2013. Print. 50.
2. Ibid. 55.
3. Ibid. 366.
4. Ibid. 16.
5. Ibid. 249.

INDEX

ABOUT THE AUTHOR

Susan E. Hamen has written more than 20 books on a wide array of topics, including the Wright Brothers, World War II, astronomy, James Cameron, and ancient Rome. Her book *Clara Barton: Civil War Hero and American Red Cross Founder* made the American Library Association's 2011 Amelia Bloomer Project Book List. Hamen lives in Minnesota with her husband and two children. She loves traveling with her family throughout the United States and exploring national parks and historic sites with each trip.